gundermann

East Germany's Coal Miner Rock Poet

david shirreff

Crunch
BOOKS

To Conny

Published in 2023 by Crunch Books, 68 Boileau Road, London SW13 9BP

www.crunchbooks.com

Cover design by Bookconsilio
www.bookconsilio.com
Cover photo credits:
IMAGO/Robert Michael(Gundermann)
Shutterstock/Sabina Schaaf (excavator)

A CIP record for this book is available from the British Library

ISBN: 978-0-9932969-6-3

acknowledgments

I am grateful to Conny Gundermann for filling some important gaps in the narrative and to the many Gundermann fans who have given their support to this project.

I would like to thank Adam Preston and Valerie Potter for making the book more readable, and Dave Robb for his generous collaboration in translating the songs.

foreword

What Gundi means to me

In 2018 I visited the Lausitz mining area of east Germany to research a book featuring Germany's filthiest industry—the production and consumption of lignite coal. I ran into two surprises: first, that the industry has its own poet laureate, Gerhard Gundermann; second, that an Englishman had got there before me—Michael Gromm, who had attempted to save one village from obliteration by strip mining.

Sadly, both protagonists are dead. But those two lives inspired me to dig more deeply, using their stories to get closer to the character of the region. Initially, I wove the two stories together, although there is no record that they ever actually met. Later, I decided to write two separate narratives.

Here is the first book—an attempt to explain Gerhard Gundermann (nicknamed Gundi) to those who didn't grow up in the region, and to those who don't necessarily speak German.

Gundi is complex. Many of his songs are difficult to understand. His life was full of contradictions: he believed in the socialist system, but rebelled against its idiocies; he drove a giant mining machine, yet wrote songs about fighting pollution; he spied for the Stasi (East German State Security) while others employed by the Stasi spied on him. After the Berlin Wall came down he continued to see some good in the fragile socialist culture that was being drowned by West German capitalism. For many stranded East Germans he was a tribune of the people.

Beyond the life story is the magic of Gundi's songs. He was no obvious rock star, but the poetry and the clarity of his voice make the words of every song as important as the music. He was truly a rock poet: some have called him the miners' Bob Dylan.

The challenge for me has been to make Gundi more accessible to the English-speaking world. As well as exploring his life I have attempted to catch the spirit of his songs in translation—some in collaboration with Dave Robb, a musicologist and singer who studied in East Germany and teaches at Queen's University Belfast.

I hope you will enjoy this book and spread the message about Gundermann further.

a note on the songs and translations

Where I quote songs by Gerhard Gundermann and others I have done so in my own English translation. The translations, like Gundi's idiosyncratic originals, have no capital letters or punctuation. Wherever possible I have tried to recreate the rhythm and rhyme structure and the spirit of the verses, rather than do a literal translation. I decided to do this in the hope of bringing these songs to a wider non-German-speaking audience. I am grateful to Dave Robb for his collaboration on some of the translations.

one

. . .

Gundi—Circa 1980

GERHARD ENJOYED HIS WORK. From a steel and glass cabin thirty metres above the ground he controlled the bucket-wheel excavator, each bucket the size of a small house. The giant machine, nearly two hundred metres long, dug deep into the sandy soil, dumping every shovel-load onto a conveyor belt, which fed the spoil onto a 'bridge', the biggest piece of moving machinery in the world. The bridge, in its turn, carried the spoil another five hundred metres behind the pit face and spewed it out at three different levels.

Gerhard worked the excavator downward to a dark seam of lignite, about three metres thick, which ran for miles at a depth of thirty metres below the surface. To get at this narrow seam, the huge shovels cut an open swathe six kilometres wide through the Brandenburg landscape. Villages, farms, ponds, orchards, streams and forests, even churches and graveyards had all succumbed over the months and years. Two other machines like Gerhard's were also at work along the six-kilometre stretch. Behind them they were leaving a wasteland more like a moonscape than anything on earth. Running beneath the machines was a railway track, which carried wagons of coal a few kilometres north to Jänschwalde, the third biggest power station in Germany. It was always hungry for more coal, its nine cooling towers belching steam into the black night.

Gerhard liked to work the night shift, alone in his steel cocoon, surrounded by the clattering of the machinery. In those rhythms and crescendos he found what he was looking for: metres and melodies for his songs. Nightly he filled up his tape-recorder, added descants above the noise of crashing steel. And in the morning he usually found something—a mixture of night owl philosophy and gritty ballad—to feed his rock band, called, appropriately Brigade Feuerstein. (Firestone being the local dialect name for lignite, or brown coal.) Lignite was the commodity that had been turning this region Lusatia (the Lausitz) upside down since the 1920s. 'God created the Lausitz,' the saying went, 'and the Devil put coal under it.'

Gerhard Gundermann—Gundi to his friends—was one of those in league with the Devil. He was a pragmatist, and a loyal citizen of the communist German Democratic Republic (GDR). If they needed someone to dig the dirty coal out of the landscape then he wanted to be the one who did it most efficiently. He was a perfectionist. He would rather drive his excavator than play cards in the canteen. He was friendly enough, but not unduly sociable—until he got home and started his second job.

Gundi led a double life, a coal miner by day, a poet, guitarist, singer and band-leader during the other waking hours, which also included long drives between concerts. He reckoned he could survive on a mere two-and-a-half hours' sleep every day.

Gundi was born in Weimar in 1955. When he was twelve the family moved to nearby Hoyerswerda, a typical East German dormitory town. The suburbs were dominated by rectangular blocks of prefabricated apartments known as Plattenbauten. Nobody was starving. Everyone had a job. Life was simple as long as you stayed out of politics and didn't go spying on your neighbour.

The year of the move he joined his school Singing Club. At the age of fifteen, he got his first guitar and was soon strumming the chords of *The House of the Rising Sun.* The Animals, Bob Dylan, Bruce Springsteen and Joan Baez shaped his musical efforts over the next few years and at seventeen he started writing his own songs.

During the summer he worked as a lifeguard at the local open-air pool. He also had ambitions to serve in the National People's Army and he enlisted at the Officers' Training School at Löbau, fifty kilometres away. But he found he was unsuited to the military. His company commander accepted him only as a leader of his own musical band. He had no aptitude either as a political officer—the National People's Army was full of them—or a tactical one. "At target practice I was so short-sighted I couldn't hit a single disc," Gundi said later. But the last straw as far as his bosses were concerned was his refusal—at a 7th October Parade celebrating the founding of the GDR—to allow his band to greet the Defence Minister, war hero General Heinz Hoffmann, with his own special song: That Was Our Comrade General. Gundi and his fellow musicians dismissed the idea as "too stupid for words". He was later judged 'not suitable' for military duties and sent home.

In March 1975, now a lanky twenty-year-old, he looked a little goofy with his protruding front teeth and huge spectacles. He loved to clown around. But underneath he was fiercely ambitious, both for his music and for some kind of role in socialist East Germany. He became a trainee mine-worker at the local lignite mine, Tagebau Spreetal, cleaning and servicing the vast machines that were ripping up the landscape near his home. In his first songs he already saw himself as a hardened warrior ready to fight for the local community.

i am an ancient man of war
grey is my hair and long
i ride upon my tired horse
the dusty path along.[1]

. . .

At twenty-two he joined the ruling Socialist Unity Party (Sozialistische Einheitspartei Deutschlands—SED) because he believed in the political machinery of the socialist state. He wanted to contribute as a responsible citizen and a worker, not just as a musician, which he didn't see as his real job.

The following year, 1978, he gained his certificate enabling him to drive one of the giant mining excavators and took over responsibility for the 170-metre long Schaufelradbagger No. 1417, built in 1959—only four years younger than himself and still shovelling.

Gundi's band at the Singing Club in Hoyerswerda now called itself the Brigade Feuerstein. It was part theatre group, part band, playing out fairy tales in front of children. Gundi, with his collarless shirt and jeans held up by braces, floppy hair and painted face behind owlish glasses, clowned about the stage as much as he sang, clucking like a chicken, pretending to eat huge slices of cake, playing the Pied Piper.

Gundi made his mark at the Singing Club by writing songs and dialogue. He brought wit and energy to the dramas and fairy tales. "I want to be something between a clown, a writer and a director," he explained at the time.

Conny was a member of the band. With her big dark eyes, round face and enchanting figure she was a delight onstage. Gundi had been in love with her since they first met at school, when she was twelve and he thirteen.

Since they were neighbours they often used to walk home from school together. They had intense conversations and imagined the same adventures: they were almost inseparable. Gundi wrote in his diary about his secret love for her.

But as they grew older and thought of settling down, Conny could not quite imagine Gundi—gangly, gauche with his protruding teeth and intellectual arrogance—as the ideal partner she had in mind. She chose Wennie, another member of the Brigade Feuerstein, and married him.

If Gundi was heartbroken he didn't show it. He found ways of staying close to Conny, helping her and Wennie in their family apartment. When children came along—Yvonne and Steffen—he was almost a second father.

Gundi had girlfriends and he would discuss them with Conny. He got one of them pregnant, resulting in a son, Martin, but the relationship didn't last and, after a couple of years, he saw less and less of his little boy.

Conny was reasonably happy with their domestic arrangement. She, Wennie and Gundi made music with Brigade Feuerstein and at home, and continued to entertain each other. Gundi had resigned himself to being the lovable uncle.

Then, one day, something happened that seemed to threaten Conny's happiness. Gundi told her about a new girlfriend—one of her school friends. It seemed to be getting serious.

Conny flew into a panic. It dawned on her that this lanky, goofy, brilliant clown meant more to her than she had allowed herself to think and she saw that she was in danger of losing him.

Conny struck. The next time the couple found themselves alone together their innocent horseplay turned into something else. Gundi's reaction confirmed what she had always known—that he was, and had always been, madly in love with her.

It wasn't long before Wennie learned their secret. They came to a sensible arrangement: Gundi moved into the family apartment, and Wennie took over Gundi's bachelor pad.

There was no rancour, but the situation became tense within Brigade Feuerstein. In the end Conny and Gundi left the group. A year later, they got married.

Conny went into her second marriage with her eyes open. She knew Gundi was the right man for her, but she had to accept that his restless energy would not let him settle down.

Something was always driving him to do more. It may have been his response to the wrath of his father, who hadn't spoken to him since he was eleven. A single incident had driven a wedge between them.

His father, a toolmaker, used to keep a pistol as a souvenir from wartime France in the drawer of his bedside table. One day, Gundi found it and decided to show it to his schoolmates. He stuffed it down his tracksuit trousers and swaggered about the playground. He certainly impressed his friends but also caught the attention of the teachers and the police. His father was arrested and given a suspended sentence for possessing a firearm. Since then he and Gundi had never spoken, though Gundi constantly thought about his father.

One night in the cabin of giant excavator 1417, deep into the late shift, he remembered that incident and the feeling of power the cold metal had given him. He imagined Special Agent Gundi, with twelve marks in his pocket, a loaf of bread, a map and a revolver on a mission to Saigon via Hamburg and Paris. That turned into a song, Colt 08:

when I was 14 found an '08 in a drawer
guess my old man brought it home from the war[2]

During his fantasy mission, things go wrong: he is stopped at the first border crossing and thrown into jail.

Conny tried to understand the demons that drove Gundi to play at concerts far into the night as both lead singer and guitarist, and then, after barely two hours' sleep, set off to do a shift driving the giant excavator. Both jobs demanded energy and adrenalin. Surely he was burning the candle at both ends. If he had been really tough she might have worried less, but he often seemed so vulnerable, like the flying fish out of water in one of his songs:

please don't squish
i'm just a flying fish
if i jump into view
don't hug me to you[3]

two

. . .

Digger Driver

WHILE GUNDI WAS TRYING to work things out with Conny, he found his new job driving the excavator tougher than he'd anticipated. His predecessor on excavator No. 1417 had left him performance targets that were initially well beyond him. He began to understand what a huge job he had taken on. Operating a giant excavator involved a team of around twenty people. They included mechanics and engineers, electricians, number-crunchers and a handful of manual workers—men and women armed with brooms and shovels, toiling through the night to make sure the coal scooped out by the bucket-wheel was free of sand. Sand in the machinery caused damage and delay.

The driver had to co-ordinate the team by radio—his only superior being the shift manager. Some of his workmates saw Gundi's defensive mask of self-assurance as arrogance and they jibed at him constantly. It took him a while to win their respect

Moreover, as with almost everything in East Germany there was the political side, even for an excavator driver. You did your job according to the principles of the GDR. You were a vital cog in the economic machine, providing heat and light to factories, workshops and thousands of people. A mistake could cost millions; on the other hand, efficient shovelling could save the nation thousands. If the team missed their monthly quota they risked having their wages docked. The quotas were inflexible: no excuses were accepted whatever the weather or the geology. When a mudslide at Bärwalde, a neighbouring mine, caused a two-week halt in production, the excavator driver committed suicide.

Gundi was eager to learn on the job, but he was not one to blindly obey orders. When he disagreed with his bosses he found it hard to keep his mouth shut. It was the same with the ruling party the SED. Within a year he was criticising the way decisions were made and was threatened with expulsion. In his own view his behaviour wasn't arrogant: he believed he could improve the world around him, changing the way the party was run, the way the state was run, and the way Brigitta, the open cast mine, was run.

Working there was physically dangerous. One accident affected him deeply: the death of Helmut, a fellow miner. He recalled it in a piece of theatre describing a funeral procession at the mine. A hearse is driven into the muddy mine workings to collect the mashed remains of Helmut.

'The hearse runs beside me, Ginzo ahead driving the caterpillar to stop the hearse getting stuck; under the conveyor belt of the excavator is a small heap with a flat iron stuck into it, and to the side lies what is left of Helmut, a lifeless glove puppet, his head looking like a hand brush.'

The threat of expulsion from the SED was commuted to a 'severe reprimand'. But the truce didn't last long. His membership of the party didn't fit with his tendency to lash out. One day at the mine he had an open row with his boss, the leader of the Brigade Rote Stern. He threw a fist at him and knocked him down.

Gundi was expelled from the SED, but he kept his job. Despite his big mouth and fiery temper his colleagues by then couldn't fault his competence and dedication. And for the mining company he had become a useful mascot: the singing digger driver. Film maker Richard Engel made a TV documentary about him in 1981. But East German television delayed showing *Gundi Gundermann* for two years and even then gave it a late night slot. "A good film, but the wrong man," said the TV bosses at the time.

Gundi's questioning of authority was part of his nature. Political criticism was an important part of the musical theatre performed by Brigade Feuerstein. But in East Germany in the mid-1980s citizens were never far away from surveillance by the Ministry of State Security, the Stasi. The Stasi kept minute records on everyone. They had a network of informers, called 'unofficial collaborators', paid to spy on their friends, neighbours and colleagues at work. They were expected to report on conversations or activities detrimental to the socialist state, unusual journeys, covert affairs, sexual preferences and the like. The most improbable people were recruited, including for a time Gundi himself. In 1977 he agreed to report on his fellow musicians when they went on foreign trips. He became an unofficial collaborator with the codename 'Grigori'. There seemed no harm in what his spymasters were asking him to do. But by 1984 he was thoroughly disillusioned by what the Stasi stood for: its harping on personalities and personal weaknesses, rather than the security of the state, its bullying tactics and its use of intimidation and physical violence. Also by that time Gundi himself was being spied on. A colleague had objected to HoyWoy, a song he had written about Hoyerswerda, his home town.

hoywoy to you we're true
    pale flower in the sand
    heat noise dust and concrete view
    you fairest city in the land.[1]

That was enough to suggest disloyalty to the Communist regime. His workmate denounced Gundi to the Stasi, which responded by stepping up surveillance of the singer and his songs. In disgust, Gundi ended his own work as a Stasi informer.

Gundi may have had thoughts about revolution but in his habits he was deeply conservative. He wore the same clothes day in, day out: jeans with red braces and the collarless 'butcher's' shirt.

He told an interviewer in the mid-1990s: "By the standards of the well-to-do, I'm poor, but by my own standards I feel I'm seriously rich. I have a roof over my head, in a terrace house that was dirt cheap, I have a family and we have food, drink and something to wear. In summer when we look out of the window we see trees. I'm world champion at lowering expectations. Most of all, I like to wear my father's old shirts dating back to 1923. I need very little; I need my music, a spoon, a cup, and everything must be in its place. Period."

Part of the essential gear was a tin case which he showed the interviewer:

"I always carry my tin case with me. So, look here: spectacle-spray, knife, fork and spoon (they were my father's), a wire-cutter, a plumber's wrench, a tape measure, a teaspoon, a small mains tester, a ballpoint pen, two penknives, a skeleton key, a nail cleaner, a lighter, a large knife to cut through rubber at work. Then this compartment for occasional items: a sandwich box, lemon-balm teabags, salt cellar and pepper mill (they were my father's in the War); over here I usually have a bottle of mineral water with a tin cup; and here's my sort-of desk compartment: notebooks, an auto manual, a pencil, a dictaphone. That's my survival pack." [Interview with Hans-Dieter Schütt in *Neues Deutschland* 24.02.1996]

Gundi was on a mission, requiring him to keep his survival pack with him at all times. Despite the rift with his father, he still wore his father's old shirts and used some of his wartime kit. In his youth he had dreamed of being a scuba-diving spy. Now he was still the outsider on his own secret mission.

In those days the family had no car: neither he nor Conny had a driving licence. To get around that problem, Gundi bought a motorbike and sidecar. The MZ ETZ 250 offered freedom, but it had its downside. Often the four of them—two children in the sidecar with Conny riding pillion—were caught in the rain. On one notable trip to Berlin they battled for five hours through storm after storm. In his brief biography, Gundi noted laconically: '1985—relationship with motorbike and sidecar'. The rainstorm experience spurred Conny on to pass her driving test. When she did, they bought their first car, a beaten-up Moskvitch in regulation pale blue. Gundi soon passed his test too.

He began to make solo appearances as a singer/songwriter all over East Germany. He also rejoined Brigade Feuerstein and wrote some of his most political songs for their shows Lebenslauf (1985), Männer, Frauen und Maschinen (1986) and Entdeckungen (1988).

At the annual Chanson festival in Frankfurt-an-der-Oder in 1987 he won first prize, though the jury had actually voted for somebody else, Stefan Körbel. The president of the Committee for The Entertaining Arts Gisela Steineckert decided against Körbel for "political" reasons. Gundi, it seems, was still tolerated politically, despite his problems with the Party and the Stasi.

The prize gave him the chance to record his first album, also called *Männer, Frauen und Maschinen,* with AMIGA, a branch of the state record company VEB Deutsche Schallplatten. Because Gundi was not that well known, and because he spent most of his life on the digger rather than giving concerts, the record did not sell well. Half of the pressing of ten thousand vinyl discs was sold to Russia for scrap.

three

. . .

Die Wende

IN 1987 CONNY and Gundi saw a chance of moving out of HoyWoy, with its concrete apartment blocks, to a house in the country.

Conny spotted a house in Spreetal sixteen kilometres north-east of the town, which she heard was becoming vacant. She and Gundi were able to swap their three-room apartment in Hoyerswerda for the terrace house with a large garden in Spreetal.

Most of the other villagers were connected with the mine at Spreetal-Nord and the power station at Schwarze Pumpe. Despite the mining to the west and the smoke plume from the power station to the north, the hamlet itself was a haven of tranquillity for the couple and Conny's two children, Yvonne and Steffen, aged fourteen and eleven. They promptly added to the family: a dog, Lisa von Lügenstein, and three cats, Sascha, Tanja and Wasja.

The couple had no idea about life beyond an urban apartment. They quickly made a mess of the garden, ripping precious plants out of what they failed to see was a rockery. They nearly poisoned themselves with their first attempts at lighting the coal-burning stove.

Across the road to the north lay woodland; to the south was a wasteland left by strip mining. But in his garden Gundi could relax. You could still hear the far-off rattle of the giant bucket-wheel excavator, but it was gentle, like the sound of a distant railway. Gundi imagined he was an astronaut returned from a mission to Mars, his head still full of vectors and calculations, but safe now. He had survived the night shift in his space capsule and could catch some sleep before tonight's concert. The lines of one song went through his head, without making much sense:

blue and blue
  the sky was so blue
  the birds and planes and we knew it too[1]

Lisa von Lügenstein stretched out in the shade, Sascha the tomcat stalked a blackbird, and Conny was in the kitchen ironing a mound of children's clothes.

But just as their home life was settling down, the country was going through rising political turmoil. Every Monday the demonstrations in Leipzig, 150km to the west, were getting bigger. Crowds thronged the square outside the Nikolaikirche where Christoph Wonneberger, a dissident pastor, led prayers and protest against the government.

Gundi was one of a privileged group of artists, mainly musicians and actors, whose criticism of Erich Honecker and his regime was quietly tolerated. From February 1987 Gundi appeared every year at the international Festival of Political Song in Berlin. The handful of East German songmakers performing there were like court jesters, allowed to poke fun at their masters as long as they didn't go too far.

Gundi was writing songs for a group called Silly and together they released an album, *Februar*, in early 1989. One track, SOS, portrays the GDR as a leaky ship with an idiot crew heading for an iceberg at full speed:

. . .

we're sailing the seven seas
in an ill-found ship of fools
our golden flag laughs in the breeze
and below us lie jet-black shoals[2]

Gundi was increasingly politically engaged. He gave a speech at an entertainment industry conference in March 1989 on the industry's capacity to push for reform, using the example of the Soviet Union's new openness under Mikhail Gorbachev. In September Gundi was among the songmakers who, before every concert, read out a political statement from the newly-formed protest party Neues Forum. It included the words:

'We want a free, self-confident people who act with a sense of community. We want a state free of violence, finger-pointing and spying. We want idlers and loud-mouths to be stripped of power, while we protect the socially weak and vulnerable'.

The pressure on the authorities during that autumn increased every week. On September 11th Hungary opened its border to allow thousands of East German 'tourists' to cross into Austria. Meanwhile thousands more were seeking refuge in the Federal German embassies in Prague and Warsaw. Sealed trains containing these East German refugees were sent from Prague and Warsaw through East Germany to the Federal Republic.

On October 2nd East German police broke up a routine Monday demonstration in Leipzig. The government stopped granting visas for travel to Czechoslovakia, which was the main escape route for East German refugees to travel on through Hungary and Austria to freedom.

On October 7th celebrations for the fortieth anniversary of the founding of the GDR, attended by Mikhail Gorbachev, served as a focus of protests which were brutally broken up by police. Over a thousand arrests were made. In Hoyerswerda, Hans-Eckhardt Wenzel and Steffen Mensching, satirical songsters in the style of Berthold Brecht and Kurt Weill, were performing their show *Da*

Da eR when Stasi officers burst in and arrested them. They were held in jail overnight. However, two weeks later, they were playing again at the Academy of Arts in central Berlin in a satirical revue known as the *Red Revels*. Gundi was on the same programme.

On October 18th party chairman Erich Honecker, the party leader since 1971, resigned. The SED was still the ruling party, though new parties such as the Greens, the Social Democrats and Neues Forum were beginning to take shape. Egon Krenz, Honecker's heir apparent, flew to Moscow at the end of October to confer with Gorbachev. He returned with promises of regime change. A dozen top party officials resigned, including the long-serving Stasi chief Erich Mielke. Restrictions on travel to Czechoslovakia were lifted.

Gundi, along with most East Germans, had no idea how fluid the situation had become. At a concert in the Magnus-Club in Berlin on October 23rd his mind was more occupied by American history than the situation at home. It was a concert he called *Memory of the Future* during which he imagined he had time-travelled to America in 1856 and the 1870s, just before and after the civil war. He related a dream: outside his house in Spreetal at midnight, while walking the dog, he had stepped into a time-tunnel and met Carl Schurz. Carl Schurz was a legendary figure, who had been born in the Rhineland in 1829, fled the country after involvement in the 1848 Revolution, first to England then America, was caught up in Republican politics, fought as one of Abraham Lincoln's generals in the Civil War, and ended up as a US senator. For Gundi it seemed quite natural to encounter this man, more than eighty years after his death, in the Spreetal forest. After exchanging reminiscences they said goodbye and Gundi found he had picked up a bunch of Schurz's anecdotes and stuffed them in his pocket.

On November 4th there was the biggest demonstration yet on the Alexanderplatz in central Berlin. Half a million people, many bearing placards, crowded into the square. Singers and actors appeared onstage. Wenzel and Mensching sang about the new head of state, Egon Krenz. Krenz had a reputation for floating to the top without committing himself to a firm opinion.

Is this a bluff or double-bluff?
　Is he sick or in a huff?
　Waving a flag of dubious stuff?
　Faking a sore throat off-the-cuff?
　Who knows?[3]

On November 6th another demonstration in Leipzig put increased pressure on the regime to allow travel to the West and hold free elections.

Three days later the Central Committee, under great strain, decided it would prepare the ground for opening up the German-German border. The committee spokesman Günter Schabowski gave a press conference that evening. The world's press were gathered to hear how this crumbling regime would respond to the latest developments in Hungary and Austria—the flooding of GDR citizens into West Germany. Schabowski referred to an eventual opening of the border. But he had been given no instructions on the timing.

An Italian journalist asked: "When will GDR citizens be allowed to cross the border without a visa?" Schabowski shuffled through his briefing papers and said uncertainly: "As far as I can see it means immediately, without delay." The press conference erupted as reporters rushed to break the news.

That night thousands of people flocked to border crossing points in Berlin. East German border guards were unsure what to do, but they no longer had the nerve to shoot their fellow citizens. Their Alsatian dogs whined uncertainly. The power of the state had evaporated. As soon as a few people had forced their way through, the trickle became a flood. The Western side of the wall became the venue for a huge party. Souvenir hunters began hammering off chunks of the wall as tokens of a regime that had suddenly become history.

Gundi was on tour in the neighbouring state of Thüringen with a group of musicians known as the Oktoberklub. As soon as the news broke that evening, people started leaving the auditorium. Back in their hotel the group crowded around a television.

They saw people on top of the Wall. They saw impromptu music and dancing. They saw the powerless border guards allowing themselves to be hugged and kissed.

But Gundi didn't share the euphoria. He had a bad feeling that this was the beginning of a hostile takeover. The sovereignty of the GDR, for all its faults, was under threat.

The next day, he was on the early shift at the mine.

"Hey Gundi," said Walter on the bus, "now you've got your revolution. You can be the boss."

"I doubt that we'll get my sort of socialism in the end."

"What's that?"

"No more fat cats. No more snouts in the trough."

In the locker room, Karl was taking off his boots.

"Hey Uncle, have you written a song about the Wall?"

"I'm thinking of one." Actually he was thinking, this mine is about to go bust. As soon as the Wessies come here they'll sack all the party stooges, all those working for the Stasi—whoever they are. He had a pretty good idea. And even that wouldn't save it. In the face of foreign competition coal was a dying industry, it was doomed. His workmates wanted him to write about their new freedom. But he feared it wouldn't be freedom at all.

my coalmine Brigitta is busted
  the last load shipped out long before
  my digger is lying there rusted
  and the earth doesn't shake any more[4]

. . .

"Hey Uncle," said Matthias. "How long before re-unification?"

"It won't be re-unification, it will be a takeover by the Federal Republic of Germany."

"What's wrong with that? It's what we always wanted."

"It may be what we wanted. But it won't do us any good."

"We'll have fat Mercedes, dishwashers, computer games, any gadget you can think of."

"Yes," said Gundi, "a complete sell-out to Western capitalism. The triumph of egotism."

"Uncle, you think socialism's better?"

"It could be." For Gundi, the fall of the Berlin Wall might have been an opportunity to create a better, fairer state with a free exchange of principles between West and East. But he didn't expect Matthias to understand that.

He put on his boots and his helmet, took his tin case and caught the transport to the digger. There it loomed in the false dawn, floodlights glaring, the Eiffel Tower framework stretching horizontally out of sight. The claws of the bucket wheel glinted in the floodlights, tearing at the coal-face and spewing hard brown clumps onto the conveyor belt. An iron ladder led Gundi to the driver's cabin where Dieter was preparing to hand over the controls.

"Heard about the Wall?" asked Gundi.

"What wall?" said Dieter. "Of course I've heard about the bloody Wall. We stopped the machines for ten minutes and danced a jig." Gundi sat in the driver's seat and laid his tin case beside him. He checked the indicator levels, oil pressure, amperes, fuel, engine revs, cutting angle. When he was satisfied with the settings and saw that the digger was running effectively he opened his tin case and took out the cassette recorder.

'My coalmine Brigitta is busted....' He fitted the words to the rhythm of the giant machine, the turning of the bucket wheel, the melody in his head.

There followed a month of demonstrations in all the main cities, demands from students, the formation of new parties, apologies and warnings from the old guard, and promises from West German Chancellor Helmut Kohl that a switch from East German Marks to West German Deutschmarks would follow any sign of democratic reform, free elections and a halt to the mass exodus to the West. Hungary and Czechoslovakia were also treading their own path to reform. On November 16th the newly declared Republic of Hungary applied to join the Council of Europe. A week later the Communist Party leadership in Czechoslovakia resigned. Dissident Czech playwright Vaclav Havel became Chairman of the newly-formed Civic Forum party, and was voted in as President soon thereafter.

four

. . .

Tribune

GUNDI THREW himself into the political debate. His biggest concern was that the GDR would lose its identity and become just a province of the capitalist Federal Republic. There were so many signs that this was already happening. West German goods were forcing less colourful East German brands off the shelves. Vans laden with luxuries and colourful trash from the West took town and village squares by storm. Street vendors tossed bananas through the air to draw the crowds. Peddlers and opportunists from all over the world came in to relieve the naïve citizens of their savings in a currency that was fast losing value.

Gundi had never been much interested in amassing material things. With his house and garden in Spreetal, his family, his job and his music, he was personally quite content. But he was concerned with the way things were going. He had never lost his belief in socialism and the goal of the common good rather than personal gain. He decided to stand for election to the new People's Chamber, the Volkskammer, as a member of the United Left Party. His concerts were his political platform. At the election in March 1990 the United Left received only twenty thousand votes, about 0.18 percent of the poll. It sent just one member,

Thomas Klein, a dissident former mathematician, not Gerhard Gundermann, to the new, free parliament in Berlin.

In the same month, Leipzig had its Spring Trade Fair, the traditional shop window for East German industry. Gleaming tractors, turbines, precision tools and even computers were on display in the crowded halls as usual. But this year it was different. The big beasts of West German industry were there in force: Gerhard Cromme head of Krupp, one of the world's biggest steelmakers; Carl Hahn head of Volkswagen, maker of Audi and Porsche as well as VW cars; Hilmar Kopper, chief executive of Deutsche Bank, Germany's biggest. In that euphoric moment before the political future of East Germany was decided, the German bosses saw Leipzig as their private hunting ground. Volkswagen would take its pick of the East German car industry; Krupp would help itself to any useful steel smelters; Deutsche Bank would take over branches of the state-owned Staatsbank. Even if they were acquiring assets just to shut them down, they were making sure that non-German rivals were at the back of the queue. The filleting of the German Democratic Republic by the West had begun.

Gundi focused on his songs. At a concert in Berlin on April 30th he sang one which seemed to incapsulate the German-German phenomenon, Stoneland:

we didn't plan it
we didn't own it
but we've already sold it
we've scoffed it and drunk it
already forgotten it
yet have no other home[1]

Another song was based on a quotation from Stalin: "Hitlers come and go, but the German people and the German state remain."

. . .

we cast our vote
so they stuffed up our mouths
they put our hands in the fire
so we couldn't slap their wrists
they pulled out our teeth
we turned a blind eye
we laid our balls on the table
and they fucked us up the arse

leaders come
leaders go
but the German people remain—dumb[2]

Gundi still felt he was a loyal citizen of the GDR five months after the fall of the Berlin Wall. He told his concert audience: 'I still have a car sticker which says 'Friend of the GDR People's Army'.' But his idea of an army was green rather than red—one there to save the planet rather than fight invaders.

our foe is wasteland
our friend every tree
a spotless strand
is our fantasy
against burning sun
and winter's freeze
we wave the flag
for the green army[3]

For once Gundi's mood was optimistic. He was an early eco-warrior, despite working in a coal mine, and driving a machine which itself used up a quarter of the coal energy it produced. Peter Rocha, a film maker, interviewed him that year for a documentary about the East German mining region, called *The Pains of Lusatia*.

"A short time ago," said Gundi, "I was in a plane and we couldn't land in Berlin because of fog. So we headed for Dresden and for the first time I flew over this landscape. It was terrible, I mean the holes...and between them the cooling towers aimed like cannons at the sky."

The Lausitz region was marked by four great scars in the landscape, the open cast mines of Welzow-South, Reichwalde, Nochten and Jänschwalde. The top forty metres of the earth's crust had been stripped and laid bare at the rate of thirty square kilometres a year for over half a century. Behind the great machines that Gundi and others drove lay an ever widening moonscape that would take decades to restore. Sterile fields and bitter lakes would need years of treatment before farmers and fishermen, wild flowers and animals could enjoy their old habitat again, if ever.

Not surprisingly when Gundi—after this shock—came to write a song about what Ought To Be, as well as dreams of a flying carpet and a magic horse he added that:

...the hole in heaven shall close again
and the holes in the earth also
don't ask me how...[4]

But his concern about the environment didn't dampen his zeal as a digger driver. He saw himself as an extension of machine No. 1417: the driver's cabin was the head and he was the brain, for eight hours a day. "When we part at the end of the shift we've experienced something together, worked well together and tested each other," he told an interviewer. "The digger must have a soul. The older it gets, the more tales it has to tell, like trees or old people.

"The irony is, when I'm driving my digger, it's shaking the foundations of the very house I live in. We miners are sawing off the branch we're sitting on." That thought inspired Keep Going, a song encouraging Planet Earth to hold firm, despite the damage inflicted by mankind:

keep going if you can stand it
    you're a smart princess
    you're a seasoned planet
    we're making you such a mess[5]

Gundi saw himself as a warrior, a temporary enemy, standing on the battlefront of the environment.. But giving up his job would solve nothing. "For me the point is that the place where I live, my homeland, should be heated as effectively as possible. Meanwhile, I'm encouraging other people with brains to find a solution so that we don't have to go on digging out coal."

That seemed to let him off the hook. He could go on driving his big machine as a source of poetic inspiration. Gundi's world, seen from the cabin of No. 1417, was one of fantasy figures: dragons, samurai, Sir Lancelot, a black galleon flying through space and time. It was a universe conceived and beaten into rhyme in that cabin suspended between heaven and earth.

Meanwhile the GDR was changing around him and about to vanish. On July 1st there was currency union with West Germany and the nation's near worthless Ostmarks became Deutschmarks overnight. Suddenly Gundi and Conny had the power to buy Western consumer goods: food mixers, radios, a decent guitar. Not that they needed much in their rustic home. Nor did Gundi have great ambitions to travel. Many of his countrymen felt a powerful need to catch up on the foreign travel they had been denied. Gundi had been to Cuba, Sweden, Paris and a handful of other places, but he was more a traveller of the mind. His fantasy could carry him into space, onto the mean streets of Atlantic City and into the armour of Sir Lancelot or an ageing samurai.

But he was not happy with the swallowing of East Germany by the Federal Republic. The negotiations were conducted less between Chancellor Helmut Kohl and his weak Eastern counterpart Hans Modrow, than between Kohl and the heads of the four Allied Powers who technically still had sovereign power in Berlin: George Bush senior, Margaret Thatcher, François Mitterrand and Mikhail Gorbachev. For the three Western powers the main goal was that East Germany should become part of NATO. For the Soviets it was the need for money to build barracks back home for the half-million or so Soviet troops and their dependents still stationed in East Germany. Once that been thrashed out East Germany could be rushed to the altar of re-unification. The Day of German Unity was scheduled for October 3rd 1990.

On the eve of unification, Gundi and Conny were driving back from a concert in Freiberg. Over the radio they heard the East German national anthem being played one last time:

'Out of ruins now arisen
With the future in our hand
Let us serve without division
Germany our fatherland'.

Gundi stopped the car. They listened to the dying strains of the anthem then the roar of the crowd at the Brandenburg Gate. But for them there was little cause for celebration. Mixed with the euphoria of freedom was the knowledge that the comfortable world they had lived in since they were born was crumbling. No more paternalistic television broadcasts. They were totally without guidance, apart from a government six hundred kilometres away in Bonn. They wept softly in each other's arms as the Mercedes and BMWs flashed by on the motorway, blasting their horns as if Germany had won another World Cup final. Conny and Gundi felt very alone.

five

. . .

Lean years

BUT AT HOME in Spreetal with Lisa von Lügenstein, two young puppies and two cats—Sascha the tomcat having disappeared—there was some comfort.

One day Gundi found an injured hedgehog in the middle of the road. He took it home, fed it and nursed it, but sadly after a couple of days he found it dead with maggots eating its eyes. To cheer himself up he went to his video collection and took out a film called *Peggy Sue Got Married*, which involved time travel. The message of the film heartened him somewhat: even if you know, because you've already lived the future, that you will fail at something—in this case a musical career—you should still give it your best shot.

Gundi still had his job. He was in demand for concerts. Life would go on. But Gundi's new songs became angrier. He felt part of a lost generation. Under Communism they had been too young and powerless to influence the gerontocracy of Erich Honecker and his Central Committee. Now the next generation, newly liberated, were already snapping at their heels. Gundi took a song, Indian Reservation, written by John Loudermilk about the Cherokee Indians, and turned it into a lament for a lost East Germany, Ossi Reservation:

. . .

the scrapheap of the Teutonic nation
this is the Ossi Reservation...

...from all the dregs that did survive
rose up a cold barbaric tribe
all politicians keep dead still
they're turning merrily on the grill [1]

The open cast mine Brigitta was finally closed down. The giant excavators fell silent and moved elsewhere. Gundi should have been pleased, because his terraced house in Spreetal was no longer under threat, no longer shaken every day by the approaching bulldozers. But he felt regret. Losing his home to strip mining, which gave him and his family their daily bread, would have been poetic justice.

The closure of the mine didn't mean he was out of work. He moved to Scheibe, another mine, ten kilometres away.

As well as solo concerts, he had his touring band, Die Seilschaft, which he had pulled together in 1992; and he was also recording with Tamara Danz and her protest band Silly.

In the mid-summer of 1992 he played solo in the assembly hall of a school in Biesenthal, a small town twenty kilometres north-east of Berlin. He was perhaps at his most relaxed, with a small audience, playing in daylight in a hall with bad acoustics surrounded by greenery. For him it was the words that mattered, even more than the music. He played some of his most bitter numbers. He and Conny were finding life difficult now. She was pregnant. Her son Steffen and daughter Yvonne by her previous marriage had left school and were looking for work—fewer than half the kids their age could find a job. Yvonne had left the family home. The puppies had gone. So had Tanya, leaving Lisa von Lügenstein and a single cat.

Gundi wrote a song which he didn't show Conny. It came as a complete surprise to her, at a concert at the Bärenzwinger in Dresden, and it made her blood run cold.

and i can't remember
    just why i got stuck with you
    and i can't remember why

we're feeding three children and three cats too
    we don't need to skimp and save just to get through[2]

Conny felt that every man and woman in the audience was looking at her. She sat frozen in her seat, unable to move. How could he do this to her when she was sitting here three months pregnant? She was silent when they got in the car.

"What did you think about the concert?" he asked.

"What do you think I thought?"

"I don't know what you mean."

"That song, I Can't Remember."

"It's not about you," he said.

"Children! Cats! Of course it's about—us."

"It's a projection."

"Rubbish!"

"Conny. Darling. That's what artists do, that's what poets do."

"They make people a laughing stock. They ruin people's lives."

"I was imagining that I was a complete arsehole."

"That's because you are a complete arsehole. You say you used to fuck women like a bus-conductor punching tickets."

"I never did. That's a metaphor. Look at me."

"Why should I look at you?"

"Look at me. Conny. It's me, Gundi, who fell in love with you at the age of thirteen. I've never looked at another woman. Well, hardly ever."

"There. You see."

"One day you'll understand," said Gundi, "that it's a beautiful love poem."

Later, at home, they hammered away until they were exhausted and fell into each other's arms.

But it didn't cease to be a traumatic time for both of them. What was Gundi's future? How relevant were his songs in a music world that had sold out to advertising and sponsorship? Luckily his mining job gave him the independence to avoid compromising his songs or his concerts. He stuck with Busch-Funk, his East German recording label. But he still needed an audience, and his fans at home were turning increasingly to Western singers and bands, and away from music that reminded them of their years behind the Wall.

Then Linda was born. When Gundi and Conny brought their new born baby back home, his life found a purpose again. His surroundings, even trees and flowers, had new meaning. Linda was his special project. He would teach her everything about this world—perverse though much of it was—and protect her from it. He was determined to be a good father, unlike his own father who he was still unable to speak to. Gundi recognised that this tiny thing had brought light back into his life:

you've fallen into my heart
    as into an empty house
    torn open the doors and windows
    and let the daylight in and out

Perhaps she had even saved him from suicide:

. . .

my pistol lies buried
with its final round
hidden under the cherry
my feet are back on the ground[3]

At the end of October, he and Die Seilschaft, his new touring band, gave an open-air concert at Berlin Weissensee. There weren't quite the numbers experienced four years earlier when Bruce Springsteen had performed there in high summer, but it was a big morale booster for Gundermann and his band. It proved that there was an audience for songs with an edge to them from the "new provinces" of the Federal Republic.

At around this time Gundi met Manfred Maurenbrecher a West German songmaker from Berlin. They had been invited to join forces for a concert in Rheinsberg, seventy-five kilometres north of Berlin—in a pairing of east German with west German singers. The two men from different backgrounds hit it off immediately. They developed a programme of songs from their childhood. It went down so well in Rheinsberg that Maurenbrecher was invited to join Gundi's current tour.

Gundi and Maurenbrecher were kindred spirits. They spent long car journeys together—even longer because Gundi seldom drove faster than 60km per hour, to save the Planet—exchanging all manner of screwball ideas.

The collaboration lasted about a year, until the managers of Gundi's band, Die Seilschaft, put their foot down: Gundi's appearances with Maurenbrecher were distracting him from their more important concerts and tarnishing his image as an east German singer, they said.

It was during his sessions with Maurenbrecher that he developed possibly his most successful song, Longing For The Rat-Catcher.

Asked a few years later what he wanted to achieve with his songwriting Gundi said: "I'd like to be something like a filling station for losers. I'd be happy if people said that in order to live they need bread, water and songs by Gundermann."

Perhaps he came closest to that ambition when he played to workers facing redundancy in their own moribund factory. It wasn't a normal concert. Finsterwalde, like most former East German towns, was facing large-scale unemployment. All of the five big local employers had made cuts since 1990. The firms were sold at knock-down prices to Western investors, who cut labour and costs mercilessly and took early profits. The most glaring example of this was the screw and wire factory VEB Draht- und Schraubenwerk Finsterwalde. In 1991 two brothers from South Africa bought the factory, with its ornate redbrick frontage, for a single Deutschmark, with all its debts cancelled. Within a year the firm was deep in the red again and the workforce had shrunk from one thousand to two hundred and fifty. Now it was bust.

Just the time for a May Day concert in one of the idle machine-halls to cheer the workers facing redundancy. They had gathered in their overalls, along with former workmates still owed their redundancy money—altogether about two hundred people. There were two trestle tables with a few crates of beer and a placard hung across from wall to wall: 'The furnace is out in Finsterwalde'.

The audience whooped and cheered as Gundi loped into the hall with his guitar, blond hair flying. He was their man—a Kumpel, a miner, who sang to them about their woes. True to form, Gundi had a new song.

"During the early shift," said Gundi, "you hope your breakfast is going to last forever. As the clock ticks towards half-past nine you dream of escaping and lying on a white beach somewhere. Hah! But when you're jobless and your life is empty, it's the reverse: you lie on that white beach and long to be back in your old Iron Land. This song is called Breakfast Forever."

. . .

...we dreamed here in our iron land
about a white and distant strand

at five minutes to half past nine
we hoped that we could stop the time...

but then one day it really came
a wicked old fairy heard us complain
at exactly twenty-five past nine
the old works clock ticked one last time...

breakfast forever breakfast for eternity

Then he added a descant to the chorus:

the furnace is out in finsterwalde
the furnace is out in the steel plant
the furnace is out in finsterwalde
the furnace is out in our iron land[4]

The demise of VEB Draht- und Schraubenwerk Finsterwalde was predictable, given the costs of production and the difficulty of finding customers. But how about a business that eliminates the gap between production and consumption? Gundi started on one of his characteristic flights of fancy:

"One night, I was in a pub with a glass of beer in my hand, reflecting on production and consumption, and I thought, why not get in training for the day when a product no longer requires a consumer. So I took the beer and tipped it straight down the toilet.

It was perfect, from everyone's point of view: the beer ended up without any great fuss, straight in the sewerage system where it belonged; the landlord was very pleased that I was still standing at around midnight and paid him for twenty beers without a murmur."

The redundant workers of Finsterwalde were a little puzzled, especially those who knew that Gundi didn't drink beer.

He told them about his cat Wasja, the only cat left in the Gundermann household now that Sascha and Tanja had gone missing.

"I'm hoping to persuade her to stay. Since I turned vegetarian there isn't so much for her to stick around for. But she's a very good hunter. Which brings me to my next song. It's called Longing For The Rat-Catcher."

....no acid would help no poison pill
no handy rodent dispatcher
then suddenly said a loony girl
we should summon the Rat-Catcher
a pot of gold would be money well spent
to get him to join the party
give him the crown or a regiment

for down below in the excrement
the rats are back doing karate[5]

six

. . .

Samurai

OCTOBER 29TH 1993

The old Schultheiss brewery in Berlin, a red brick extravaganza, was heaving with people of all ages. A queue a hundred metres long snaked down the street. The attraction: Gundermann & Seilschaft. Although this was old East Berlin, West Berliners also flocked here to enjoy some of the more edgy post-GDR culture.

The brewery, once the biggest in the world, had stopped production in 1967. The Frannz Club, an avant-garde venue for GDR youth, sited in the old tap room, had flourished during the 1970s and 80s—Gundi had played there in 1990 with an informal group of musicians known as Die Wilderer. But later that year the Frannz Club went bust. In 1991 there were plans to convert the huge space—the size of two football pitches—and its twenty buildings, into a 'Culture Brewery' with a museum, theatre, a huge auditorium, pubs and restaurants. Several attempts failed because of troubles in the property market—a boom just after unification had quickly turned into a bust.

But the giant boiler room had already been renovated and was used for concerts. It was a fitting place for Gundi and Die Seilschaft to launch their first album together, *The Seventh Samurai.*

The title song, about a samurai destined to lay down his life for 'little' people, was a typical Gundi theme: the warrior at the ready, prepared to serve ordinary folk and risk death, expecting little or no reward. The Berliners loved it: the quirky, jumbled words that seemed only to hint at a meaning, the compelling rhythm and the refrain 'Ay-yoh' which had the whole boiler room gyrating.

a samurai sits down at your table
    to coffee, bread and marmalade
    we like to eat our meals with little people
    something we rather leave unsaid[1]

Between then and Christmas there was a frenzy of concerts, thirty-six of them up to December 22nd. Gundi used up all his annual leave from the mine. It was a time to make hay and spread the word all over Germany—Gundermann & Seilschaft were a phenomenon. Longing For The Rat-Catcher, one of the tracks on their new album, started climbing up the monthly chart of German songmakers.

When Gundi got home late on December 23rd he slept for hours before emerging to share baby Linda's second Christmas. It was a happy time. Gundi's music-making with Die Seilschaft was going well; Conny was spending more time with the children. When Gundi was at home he gave as much time as he could to Linda: in the garden, walking in the forest, with his guitar, reading to her, telling her stories. Conny worried that he was burning the candle at both ends. His colleagues at the mine did too, although they couldn't fault his competence at the job: when it came to handling the giant digger Gundi was one of the best.

Longing For The Rat-Catcher hit number one on the songmakers' chart in January, dropped to number three in February, then hit the top spot again in March. Gundermann & Seilschaft had solid fans in the former East Germany. What about the West? The concert circus continued: next up was the State Theatre in Tübingen south-west Germany.

Tübingen, home to around fifty thousand students and academics, was one of the most famous university towns in Germany. Streets of mediaeval houses led to a hilltop castle which dominated a bend in the river Neckar.

For Gundi it was like an image from his own storybook of mediaeval knights, dragon slayers and damsels in distress. He took time to wander the streets, pausing at the Stiftskirche long enough to see extraordinary carved marble tombs behind the altar: battle scenes, exotic beasts, knights in armour, all appearing to have grown out of the marble. He walked up to the castle. The streets may have been centuries old, but they were also spotless, every timber beam and cobblestone polished by years of use. He came back another way and found Mario and the others in a restaurant, die Forelle, having a long lunch.

Gundi felt like a foreigner in his own country. This was deepest Swabia but it could have been Japan—the Japan of the Seven Samurai.

They strolled over to the Landestheater on the other side of the river, unloaded the van and set up their equipment.

"It should be packed tonight," said Günther, one of the roadies.

Longing For Fhe Rat-Catcher was still top of the songmakers' chart. But strangely the theatre didn't fill up. Gundermann & Seilschaft played to an enthusiastic but small crowd.

It was disappointing, but they soldiered on. They had played empty halls before, and at least these were real fans. But they were relieved to get back home to the east.

A month later in Dresden, six thousand fans braved a rainstorm to see Gundermann & Seilschaft at the Junge Garde, an open-air stage in a large park east of the city centre. Apart from a dip to No. 3 in February, Longing For Fhe Rat-Catcher had been top of the songmakers' charts every month that year. Many of the fans knew the words. A sea of umbrellas, thoughtfully provided by the local cigarette-maker F6, rocked to the music.

Gundermann & Seilschaft had put themselves on the map. It was no big surprise when the organisers planning a Bob Dylan tour in Germany asked them to appear before him as a warm-up band.

Gundi was writing new songs. He was also trying to hold down his job as a digger driver. And now there was an urgent need for extra rehearsals.

The concert was in the open air on the banks of the river Elbe. It was a big occasion for Dylan's East German fans.

But if Gundi hoped he could make friends with Bob Dylan he was disappointed. Dylan was on his *Never Ending Tour* of the entire world. Two days ago he had been in Warsaw, two days before that in Krakow, and the day before that Prague. To Gundi it seemed as if Dylan had no idea what country he was in and what kind of people he was performing to. They were just fans who sang along to Mr Tambourine Man and It Ain't Me Babe.

But the local band Gundermann & Seilschaft did their warm-up to huge applause and then left the floor to Dylan. The great rock poet hardly acknowledged them.

"Fuck Dylan," said Gundi later. "I love his songs. His songs are more important than him. Songs are like children that you bring into the world and then let fend for themselves. You shouldn't look to the parents to understand them, you should look at the children themselves."

Twelve days later Gundi's band did the same service to another American singer Joan Baez at her open-air concert in Frankfurt on the river Oder. She was the opposite of Dylan—warm and friendly—and sang numbers with the German band.

seven

. . .

Father

IN THE MINERS' locker room, there was the usual banter.

"Anything new, Uncle?" asked Kurt.

"Nothing," said Gundi. "Oh, my father died."

His father, who Gundi hadn't seen since he was fourteen, died of a lung infection. He had always been a heavy smoker. Since the incident with the pistol they had not spoken. So Gundi was surprised that day, when he was alone in the cabin of his digger, that he wept. Real tears, recalling the frustration of all those years of not having a father, and what might have been. For the first time too, he felt sorry for his father. Disowning your son, when the brat is only twelve, is something not done lightly. He must have seen something in little Gerhard that disturbed him deeply, something that reminded him of himself at that age, a twist in his character perhaps that he had hoped he had long forgotten? All too late now to resolve.

The death came when Gundi was at the height of his career. Somehow he had managed a metamorphosis from East German rock rebel into a poet for a lost nation, a nation which no longer existed, except as a lingering piece of 'Ostalgia' in the minds of its disenfranchised people.

Many of the smart, the rich and the well-connected had abandoned their former Fatherland for the bigger prizes available in the West. Gundi had a sniff of that the previous year after Gundermann & Seilschaft's award-winning tour in the Western cities and their concerts with Bob Dylan and Joan Baez. But the audience reaction in the West—polite but detached—had taught him that his true public was at home, in Berlin, Brandenburg, and the Lausitz. There he could be himself, among his friends, his former school buddies, his fellow musicians, all of whom had grown up in the East, and his workmates, the Kumpel, who toiled with him in the mine. He felt it was their companionship that supported him now, as he wept for his father—yes, for his father and the sad, bitter life he must have led.

Gundi swung out of the cabin with a new song in his head:

father come and bake me a cake
make me whole make me young again[1]

Gundi's mother had not spoken to his father for the past ten years. She shed no tears now. When Gundi went to see her the following Wednesday she seemed lighter, more relaxed, as if finally seeing her man buried was like tying up loose ends.

"He was a bully," she said. "Now he's dead, I can tell you he used to beat me black and blue. I could never understand what I had done wrong. It was as if just being in the same house as him was a crime."

"Didn't you love him, ever?" asked Gundi.

"Of course. He was such a proud, imposing man why wouldn't you fall in love with him? When he had eyes only for me, and fought off all the opposition. But that's a million miles from how our life was together. And when you were born…" she stopped.

"When I was born?" asked Gundi.

"Good. I'll say it. He hated you. I can only explain it that way.

As if you at the age of zero, or six, or ten, were his deadly rival. He was jealous of you, his own son."

"Ha! Because I was so brilliant, and talented, and good-looking, with my goofy teeth and owlish spectacles?"

"Exactly. He could see you were a star. And he couldn't take it."

"He could see I was a clown—I am a clown. That's what he couldn't take. Me parading around the playground with his French army pistol. It was humiliating. I can see that now."

"It was long before that. You two were on a collision course from the moment you were born."

"You're exaggerating."

"No."

"Tell me about the good times."

"What good times?"

"When you were young, without a care in the world."

"Between Adolf Hitler and Erich Honecker we didn't have many good times."

"Nonsense, Mutti. What about all those tales from Oma, when you were a child?"

"It's true. My grandmother did make me happy, with her stories about the times before the Great War. Life was hard. 'But we didn't know any different,' she used to say. Beyond the village there was just Brandenburg, flat landscape for mile after mile."

"You should write those stories down."

"You write them. You're the writer." After that, Gundi started writing some things down.

Every Wednesday, if he didn't have a gig, he visited his mother and often steered the conversation to the 'olden' days before Hitler and Honecker, before Kaiser Wilhelm and the 'war to end all wars' which somehow didn't. One day, Gundi thought, he would transport himself back to those times.

eight

. . .

Unplugged

NOVEMBER 22ND 1994

Tamara Danz had masses of flaming hair. Onstage she was a lion whose flowing mane belied her sex. And her style was political rock. She and Gundi put their bands together in November 1994 for a concert entitled *Unplugged*, with twelve musicians onstage—from Tamara's band Silly, and Gundi's Gundermann & Seilschaft. They played at the Lindenpark in Potsdam to around nine hundred people.

Both singers could be wild and raucous, but also soft and gentle. To their fans, maybe, they seemed a perfect match. As they sang they knew it was an unforgettable mix of voices and minds.

They started with a song written by Werner Karma:

Remember, Father,
When you're cold:
We're equal guys.
I won't let you
And don't let me
Kill with sheer lies.[1]

. . .

They were on song. When Tamara sang Gundi's song Flying Fish, which he had written for her, she was the fish:

the water looks just like a mirror to you
you stare into it and you can't see it's me
i'll leap up for a moment into view
but any longer with you i can't be[2]

It was a poignant moment—more so because Tamara had just been diagnosed with breast cancer. She had told only a few people, and certainly the way she commanded the stage gave no indication that she was sick. Another song, which Gundi had written around 1993, One Day, took on new meaning:

one day my feet will no more fill my shoes
one day your lilac tea won't be much use
one day i'll fall into an empty space
and leave you single in this place

sometimes i'll come and see you from afar
sometimes i'll leave the cellar door ajar
sometimes a strange cat will materialise
sometimes that cat will be me in disguise[3]

And it was not hard to imagine Tamara as a cat, returning to haunt the venue after her death.

They repeated the concert on New Year's Day at the Volksbühne in Berlin. It was a sell-out but lacked the magic of the show in Potsdam. Tamara and Gundi had put their soul into that first concert. The second was performed at the insistence of Frank

Castorf, the artistic director of the Volksbühne, who was a Gundi fan. Castorf saw in Gundi "a mixture of brittleness and dilettantism.......a flavour of East German-Russian folklore".

But a dark secret was nagging at Gundi: his past role with the Stasi as the unofficial collaborator codenamed 'Grigori'. The Stasi Records Agency headed by Joachim Gauck was slowly sifting through the Stasi files that had escaped destruction. There were 111 kilometres of documents, including the files of over five million fellow citizens spied on by collaborators like Gundi. Gradually, as the victims and journalists got access to those files, stories about who had spied on whom were emerging. Gundi knew it was only a matter of time before someone discovered his 'Grigori' file and linked it to him. He had told Conny about his past collaboration. Over the years he had even dropped hints to members of the band Silly and his own Seilschaft. On one television show he had made reference to being 'one of them', that is, an unofficial collaborator, but no one picked up on it at the time.

In January 1995 two talk show hosts working for the local radio station Ostdeutscher Rundfunk Brandenburg, Jürgen Kuttner and Lutz Bertram, were suspended after it came to light that they had both collaborated with the Stasi in the 1980s. The Gauck Commission had challenged Jürgen Kuttner, while Lutz Bertram jumped before he was pushed.

When Conny heard the news she rounded on Gundi:

"You have to say something. It's only a matter of time before the Gauck people get to your file."

"What about the Stasi operations on me? I was expelled from the party for God's sake."

"These things don't cancel each other out. You reported on people. They'll read what you said about them. Maybe they were arrested or went to jail because of you. You have to make some kind of statement, sooner rather than later."

"It was chicken feed. I reported on how they behaved on foreign trips—stuff like that. Besides, we have this record deal coming through. Not a good time to rock the boat."

So he sat tight, though he dropped a few hints with his friends in the Seilschaft.

Then in April Gundi got the call he had been dreading. It was from Alexander Osang, a reporter at the *Berliner Zeitung*. Could they meet?

"Sure. I have nothing to hide," said Gundi.

Alexander came for coffee and cake in the Gundermanns' garden. It was a warm day. Lisa von Lügenstein lay under the coffee table. Linda was asleep in her buggy under the cherry tree. On the table sat three fat files which logged Gundi's activities as 'unofficial collaborator Grigori'.

"Have you read all that crap?" Gundi asked.

"Yes," said Alexander. He was a diligent reporter. He wanted to understand, without prejudice, what drove someone as intelligent as Gundermann to report on his colleagues to a state apparatus that was not much different from 'Big Brother' in George Orwell's *1984*.

"In 1976 I believed in the GDR project," said Gundi. "When two guys invited me in and asked me to 'collaborate' with the ministry I didn't hesitate. Why should I? I had been to officer training school. I was one of them."

He had reported on the behaviour of band members on foreign tours, their love lives and extra-marital affairs. It was trivial stuff, but at the time it was given huge importance.

"Now it makes me cringe," he said. "How could I have been so mean-minded? I didn't think that I might be damaging people's lives. I don't think anyone went to jail, but maybe it affected their careers."

For nearly eight years Gundi had continued to report on his fellows. Once, the Stasi sent him to Budapest to contact two West Germans who were allegedly helping East Germans to escape to the West. His mission was to lure them to a meeting in East Berlin. But Agent Grigori failed to deliver.

As he became disillusioned with the ruling party and the petty-mindedness of the Stasi he stopped filing reports. By 1984 he had been expelled from the party and his Stasi collaboration ceased. In fact he became a target of Stasi surveillance himself.

"Have you told your colleagues?"asked Alexander.

"I did ages ago, but I don't think it really sank in at the time."

"What did you say to them?"

"I remember once backstage saying 'You know you keep mentioning those arseholes who were with the Stasi? Well I was one of them for a while'.'

"How did they react?"

"Well. It was funny. They didn't really react. It was as if they knew already. They knew what sort of person I was."

"A typical Stasi collaborator?"

"No! I don't see myself like that. Yes I was an arsehole. I'm not proud of what I did. But it was a phase which I came out of in 1984. I'm more of a rebel than a collaborator."

"Will your fans see it that way?"

"It depends how I break it to them, if I get the chance, before you tell them."

Alexander agreed to hold off for a while, on condition that he was there when Gundi spoke out.

The chance came later that month. Gundi was playing solo at a club in Berlin. Alexander came. It was a small audience but Gundi was nervous: he feared that once he told them they would all walk out.

He started on the subject of astrophysics, which was his chosen theme of the evening, to be interspersed with songs.

"But before I begin I need to clarify something. Two years ago I said on a television show that I had worked for the Stasi. The audience at the time probably thought 'Yes, we all worked for the Stasi.' But now I want to put the record straight.

"I was an unofficial collaborator codenamed 'Grigori'. You can read my file. In 1984 I was thrown out of the party and stopped reporting for the Stasi. Now, looking back, I'm ashamed of what I did. But at the time I thought I was being a good citizen."

Gundi paused for any reaction, but there was stony silence.

"Now I'd like to continue the concert. If you want to walk out I'll quite understand. If you want to throw eggs, throw them at me not my fellow musicians."

Nobody moved. Nobody wanted to applaud—that would have meant approval. But nobody walked out.

He sang the first song, called Off The Leash:

all the movies i wanted to shoot have been put in the can
all the clothes i wanted to sew are already sewn
all the songs i wanted to write have been sung by the chief
i'm just a poor dog but who
ever let me off the leash[4]

As the refrain died the audience clapped. They clapped for a long time, as if they were applauding not only this new song but also Gundi's confession, and the person he now was, despite his Stasi past: he was a tribune of the people, a poet for a lost generation, a spokesman for the citizens of a state that had disappeared, the more human for being flawed himself.

Towards the end of the programme, as if to confirm his views on 'unofficial collaborators', he sang a new song about Sieglinde. A factory worker meets Sieglinde at a party, the only girl who pays him any attention. The next day, his workmates tell him she betrayed him to the Stasi, but he doesn't care:

they say you spied on me
but no one else paid me attention
like water that flows to the sea
few secrets i failed to mention

hey Sieglinde
when i find you
we'll have a ball
give me a call[5]

After the concert, Gundi spoke to Alexander:

"So, are you going ahead?"

"It's already written. It will be in the paper tomorrow."

"I hope you haven't been too tough on me."

"Look, Gundi," said Alexander, "we all had to put up with this Stasi shit. Now we have to shovel through it and get it out of our system. You weren't the worst by a long shot."

The next day Gundi drove to Hoyerswerda to pick up a *Berliner Zeitung*. Alexander was overall sympathetic, trying to explain Gundi's complex character:

"That Gundermann of all people had to have been a Stasi spy should have been obvious when you came to think of it. It was typical of him, just as it was typical of him that he would later break off all Stasi co-operation. He was gathering experience. The esoteric Gundermann would say: 'What you can't learn, you have to suffer'."

Alexander also quoted him as saying: 'Perhaps no one will want to do another concert with me. If so, I'll just wait two years and start again.'

Gundi had warned his Seilschaft band about his planned confession. Because of the hints dropped and their own intuition they really already knew. But worse than the sense of betrayal was the reality that all concerts would be cancelled, and the record deal with a West German company would be dropped. Their publicity manager, Vivi Eickelberg, decided she could no longer represent them. "After this, Gerhard no longer has a future in the West," she concluded.

Tamara Danz, so close to Gundi in spirit, especially since their last two concerts together, wanted nothing more to do with him. All her life she had been a protester. But she saw now that Gundi had always sat on the fence, part Communist stooge, part licensed dissident intellectual.

She decided to block the release of their joint recording of that magical evening.

At the end of May, Steve Koerner concluded in an article in the weekly *Die Zeit*: "The career of this singer, who still drives a digger at a mine near Cottbus—and mostly for that very reason was valued as a beacon of morality—is over. All doors that had been wide open for this forty-year-old have suddenly slammed shut."

Gundi was angry but philosophical. "Shit happens," he told Conny. But he wanted to find out what had become of his 'victims'—those he had reported on. He wrote to the ones he could find. 'Can we talk about it?' he asked. Few replied. One was a fellow musician, who he visited in Cottbus. Gundi had no memory of what he had written about this man, and the musician would not remind him: he sat back and said nothing. It was clear that he enjoyed making Gundi squirm.

During the early summer Gundi continued with his night shifts, and with writing songs. But the phone didn't ring. He had little contact with Die Seilschaft. The new album which they had been discussing appeared to be on hold.

nine

. . .

Gleitflug

SEPTEMBER 1995

Gundi and his band Die Seilschaft worked hard on their comeback. They were recording an album called *Frühstück für Immer* (*Breakfast Forever*), the title track being the song Gundi had sung in the disused factory at Finsterwalde two years earlier. But there were no concerts until September, when they appeared at the Volksbühne in Berlin with an assortment of bands including the Anglo-Irish group The Pogues. BuschFunk, the East German record company, had stuck by Gundi and in October published his first songbook with sheet music. (A perculiarity of all Gundi's published songs was the absence of punctuation and capital letters, a rule adhered to in the lyrics translated in this book..)

By November Gundi and the band were ready to release the album, and had their first concert to launch it on November 25th at the Kulturbrauerei—the Culture Brewery—to great acclaim. They performed a series of concerts between then and Christmas in Berlin, Dresden and Leipzig. *Frühstück für Immer* won the German Record Critics' prize for rock music that year. Gundi was back, but noticeably mainly in East Germany.

Most of the songs on the new album were about war, revolution, the dysfunctional workplace and social dislocation, some written in the 1980s, some new. More darkness was creeping into Gundi's lyrics, and a sense of death and destruction. One song was just called War:

yes brother that was war
who dumped it at our front door
we fought and saw each other die
i was full of hate
and didn't even know why[1]

Death and destruction, and a sense of being stuck in one place, being defined by his own geography—the Lausitz, Hoyerswerda, where he grew up and went to school and later alienated his friends. All is summed up in Here's Where I Was Born:

here's where i was born
where the cows are thin as our luck
here where my love turned forlorn
And here's where i'll win her back[2]

Gundi's big hero Bruce Springsteen embarked on a 'solo acoustic tour' of Europe in February 1996. On St Valentine's Day he performed in Dresden at the Palace of Culture.

Gundi was in the audience. He didn't have the nerve to say hallo to Springsteen, but along with thousands of fans he enjoyed the strains of The Ghost of Tom Joad.

Gundi may have had the same chords ringing in his head when he wrote one of his most haunting ballads, Coming and Going:

the ferryman comes to the shore
and on the wooden landing stage

all the pale souls stand before
the boatman takes them all away

far from hunger far from thirst
away from schnapps away from wurst
away from money off the deck
out the window off your neck[3]

A month later, Gundi was interviewed on television by Anne Will, a leading chat show host. She and a colleague grilled him on his Stasi past. He squirmed a little, not always having ready answers and taking time to think. "It's not as if, now that I'm forty, I would do everything exactly as I did when I was twenty-four." But he wasn't offering to apologise for what he did twenty years earlier —rather he attempted to rationalise his actions. And he concluded: "I got my waistcoat dirty, but not my hands."

For Gundi's loyal fans it wasn't a problem. But for Tamara Danz, now dying of cancer, it was still an obstacle to their friendship. She refused to see him.

ten

. . .

Sinkflug

IN JULY 1996, Tamara Danz was dying of breast cancer at the age of forty-three. Gundi wrote her letters, left messages with her friends, but got no reply. It was a source of great sadness to him that they were never reconciled.

The East German rock scene went into mourning for her death, added to the next month when Rio Reiser, a West German rock singer also died aged forty-six. It seemed an era was coming to an end. The lost generation, which had begun to find itself five years after the Wall came down, was losing its edge.

Gundi too was losing his sense of direction. The biggest blow came towards the end of the year when finally the giant bucket-wheel diggers stopped at the open cast mine at Scheibe where he worked. He was laid off.

The bulldozers had never got as far as the family home in Spreetal, and now he and Conny and the five-year-old Linda were living there, with a handful of neighbours, flanked by a power station and abandoned mine workings.

At first it was a blessed relief not to have to force himself out of bed for the five o'clock shift. He could take more interest in Linda and the ageing dog Lisa von Lügenstein. But when he tried to write a song there was no crash of metal on metal to fill his head with powerful tunes and hard phrases.

What he wrote now was full of nostalgia, for the mine and for his workmates. He had laboured at one open cast pit or another for twenty years and had escaped any serious accident. The miners' patron saint was St Barbara, but Gundi always felt he had his own guardian angel watching over him, as he wrote in the song Angel Above The Mine:

there flies an angel over the mine through the smoky sky
for nearly half a lifetime he's watched over me
now he's saying goodbye[1]

Gundi was jobless, looking for anything that would complement his musical career. Once he had dreamed of being a bicycle mechanic, because of his love for such an efficient, elegant and environmentally friendly machine. But there was only one bike shop in Hoyerswerda, and they didn't need an amateur assistant.

Finally, Gundi applied for an apprenticeship at a carpentry shop.

Hartmut, the manager, was sceptical:

"You really want to start an apprenticeship at the age of forty-two?"

"I need to do something with my hands besides playing the guitar. I'm an artisan."

"OK, Gundermann. You start on Monday. Let's see how long you last."

Gundi turned up and was soon called 'Uncle'. It was a nick-name they had already used at the mine, but for a different reason. There he was respected as the boffin who knew more about the theory than most of his workmates. At the carpenters shop he was seen as a late-developer, all fingers and thumbs. Yet he stuck to his workbench and was delighted when he started work on a wooden rocking-chair that he would eventually take home and show to the family.

Something was missing though. Most of the people in the workshop were on job creation schemes, putting in time so that they qualified for benefits.

It was not like being in the pit, with his guardian angel watching over him. It was a time filled with a melancholy nostalgia for what could never come back—the camaraderie of the mine, the remnants of that common experience and his times with the youthful Communist-era Red Star Brigade.

One of his compositions of the time incorporated words from the traditional Miners' Song, 'Good luck! The miner comes.' It was a salute to the time when miners brought prosperity and hope to the region, with prospects of gold and silver. But those hopes have gone, the source has dried up, and the mine 'has eaten our children'.[2]

eleven

. . .

Landung

GUNDI TEAMED up with Petra Kelling, an East German actress, to produce an evening of reminiscences about the Lausitz, based on stories told to him by his mother and the diaries of Conny's grandmother 'Oma Else'.

Petra, a Berliner, had come to love Gundi's songs. Gundi, as always, was drawn to doing something theatrical—theatre was as important to him as music. They discussed combining story telling with music. Petra came to Gundi's house and together with Conny they worked on a collection of songs and anecdotes that grew longer and longer. They estimated the performance would take three hours if they included everything they wanted.

Petra was worried that they wouldn't have time to rehearse.

"It's alright for you, Gundi, you're on your home turf and everyone knows you and your songs. But I'm just a stranger from Berlin. They won't want me next to you onstage."

"Don't be such an old woman, Petra," said Gundi, "you're a professional."

They played to a packed hall in Hoyerswerda. Gundi and Petra read snatches from the lives of the grandmothers and other Lausitz women. The anecdotes stretched from the late 19th century, through two world wars, near-starvation, Nazi dictatorship and flight in 1945 from the advancing Soviet army, to life under Soviet occupation and finally East German Communism. The tales alternated with some of Gundi's gentler songs.

'How softly Gundi is singing,' thought Petra, 'as if he's trying to shield Oma Else from harm.' She could see tears in the eyes of some of the audience. It was a big occasion, as if Gundi was giving these abandoned folk in Hoyerswerda a fresh sense of their own worth. Yes, we do count for something. Yes, we do have a history that we can be proud of: a peasant people, overrun by wars and counterwars, who have clung to their land and their heritage.

But behind Gundi's softness and gentleness there was turmoil going on inside. Tina, his drummer, a slightly built former actress, sensed it in rehearsal—when they managed to rehearse. Gundi was on edge, no longer the relaxed gunfighter or samurai swinging down from the cockpit of his giant excavator. That side of his life no longer existed. He was an apprentice carpenter and his stamping ground was a workshop on the outskirts of Hoyerswerda.

Worst of all, instead of the crashing of metal on rock and metal on metal there was hammering and power-sawing that he couldn't control, and a radio permanently tuned to 'Energy Sachsen', pumping out pop songs and advertising jingles that prevented any meaningful words or tunes from forming in his head. He had been robbed of his source of inspiration. Nothing in his power would bring it back.

"I have cupboards full of material," he told Tina in a heart-to-heart phone call, "but I can't write anything new. It's driving me crazy. I used to shout and scream in the cab and no one could hear me, nobody bothered me. Now I'm like a mouse. I feel so alone. I've had enough, I'm so unhappy."

Tina felt helpless. There was no point in telling him he should give up his job—she knew how much being a manual worker meant to him—or that he should stop writing for a while. There was probably three years' worth of songs stuffed into those cupboards, but he wouldn't be satisfied with old material: Gundi always had to be writing something new.

Luckily, when he was performing, he could shrug off all that sorrow. With the band he could clown, and when he sang solo he had become a master of rhythm and intonation. For him, the words and inflexion were all important. The guitar was melodious but secondary: the voice led, the guitar followed.

In May, Gundermann & Seilschaft played a concert in Berlin-Pankow on the open-air stage in the Schönholzer Heide. Most fans sat on the grass. A handful danced in front of the stage. Tents around the field sold beer and sausages. It was like a family occasion. But the songs they offered were mostly hard-core ballads about Fighting Like Men, War, Mining, The Devil Speaks. Only Linda, the song about Gundi's daughter, and Going Home were more tender.

Gundi seemed his normal, relaxed self onstage, but there was a deep anxiety gnawing at him. He had always been creative. Now, no new songs were coming. All the fans wanted was the old favourites. There was no pressure, no craving for something new, except within himself.

Conny knew this better than anyone. She could see the physical effect on him. He was getting thinner. She felt his heart beating within the wracked body and feared it might burst.

Olli, a girlfriend from the 1970s saw him backstage that evening. She congratulated him on how well he and the band worked together, but she saw that Gundi was deeply troubled, and gave him a hug.

"Olli, I can't go on like this," he said.

"Nonsense, you'll bounce back, you always do. The next gig will be different."

"I'll be happy if I manage one more gig." Olli felt the difference in his body, always thin but usually full of pent-up energy. It was limp and lifeless—like cotton-wool, she thought.

But the carousel went on. In early June Gundi and Conny spent three days rehearsing in Hoyerswerda for a show celebrating the 20th anniversary of the Brigade Feuerstein. Nearly all the old Feuerstein faces converged on the Kulturfabrik, the town's four-year-old Culture Factory. They caught up, talked, riffed and reminisced over those days before the grand spectacle. On the morning of June 13th the first show was *Malwina*, a play for children. Gundi clowned as he used to, prancing about with a fake polaroid camera, snapping and pulling out comic cartoon faces to distribute to the clamouring kids. For Gundi it was like coming home. The stress of the past few months slipped away. In the audience he could see familiar faces with tears flowing freely. In the bar afterwards the old guard of the Brigade Feuerstein, some with extended beer bellies, were preparing for a long night of celebration. Gundi stayed for a while, drinking his usual fizzy water. But then he and Conny had to leave. Tomorrow he had an important solo concert in Krams, nearly two hundred kilometres away.

The long drive to Krams took Gundi via crowded motorways around Berlin into the empty landscape to the north-west. It was glorious June weather. He was tired, but he knew this would be like a home game: a Sunday afternoon audience in a small village hall, with a mixture of local and loyal fans. There would be no amplification, just his voice and his favourite acoustic guitar.

And indeed he used the occasion as much to air his thoughts on life and Planet Earth as to sing songs. First up was a song from the 1980s, The Fool[1], about a travelling harlequin who three times chooses the open road rather than hitching himself to the right woman. The next, right up to date, was Road To The North, about the road he always took past the power station of Schwarze Pumpe and the new motorway to Berlin. He's not sure how he fits into his new landscape—as a former miner, or as a stranger?[2]

He looked forward to midsummer, which would be the following weekend. "Midsummer is a time when the sun reaches its zenith and has to decide whether to go on towards winter and its ultimate setting, or not. Just like me at the age of forty-two. Sometimes looking back is the best way forward."

Nearly twenty years earlier, on a midsummer's day, he had written a song about an ageing Lancelot and his ageing horse Rosinante. The knight's eyesight is going and his hair is falling out, but he's waiting for the next call to arms.

and i don't know if i can sing anymore
to touch a soul
and i don't know if i can spring anymore
before an open goal[3]

There followed two of his most beautiful songs, Grass:

ever higher grows the grass
wild and tall and green
till the scythes softly pass
in their arc so clean[4]

and One Day, which he had sung most memorably together with Tamara Danz in November 1994:

sometimes i'll come and see you from afar
sometimes i'll leave the cellar door ajar
sometimes a strange cat will materialise
and sometimes that will be me in disguise[5]

Gundi reminisced in relaxed fashion about his time as a trainee in the open cast mine. As the lowest of the low he was called the 'Occupier of the Dog Kennel'. He sang the touching song about his father, then told a story about visiting his father's grave:

"I had taken my four-year-old daughter, which was probably a mistake. 'How come they're all shut in?' she said. 'They get nothing to eat and they can't breathe.' As we got home she asked: 'Papa when are you going to die?' To which her mother said: 'We're not in such a hurry, we want to wait until you're a bit older and perhaps have a child of your own.'"

After the interval, on this long Sunday afternoon, Gundi became more expansive, airing some of his more oddball ideas. For example, a notion that there should be an 'educational planet' where children would be sent to acquire all the wisdom known to man, before they were let loose on the world. On the educational planet they would work through various social systems such as feudalism, slavery, capitalism, communism, and come back as fully formed human beings. Which planet should it be? Gundi reflected and decided on the moon, which would be close enough for parents to visit at the weekend. Then another thought struck him: O God, perhaps I'm not the first to have such an idea. Maybe, millions of years ago, somebody set up Earth as an educational planet. Which means that when you die it isn't such a bad thing: you've simply graduated.

Gundi was fairly sure mankind would mess up its own planet so much that it would eventually have to leave. "Insects," he said, "are the great adapters. Their first trick is that they have total harmony between their personal interest and the interest of the community, in fact by ignoring their own interest in favour of society: the perfect socialist state. Their second trick is limiting their own life span.

"And when we look around," Gundi continued, "we have to admit that the formula for human survival is no longer Soviet power plus electrification, which was an erroneous path, but it could be Stalinism plus Chernobyl. Stalinism could be a way of reducing personal interests to a minimum, and should we say two hundred times Chernobyl worldwide would be enough to reduce the individual life-span and raise our mutation rate, so we can adapt ourselves more quickly and give the insects more competition?"

The concert audience may not have expected such flights of fancy, but Gundi was on his own trajectory. Nobody was telling him to stop.

"Somehow the planet must get rid of us, who are trampling around so inconsiderately. So it seizes on fire, flood, AIDS and cancer. Incidentally I believe that cancer is by far the most interesting solution."

His banter was part personal philosophy, part nostalgia for his old job, which haunted him daily. "If I had gone on working at the mine I would have had to move house, because the excavator was working towards my own cellar, and sometime in the year 2002 I would have landed in my own back yard. However, Almighty God so ordained it that the excavator was scrapped and not my house. The problem with that is, not only is my house still standing, but I still have the same neighbours."

He then launched into a rowdy song about various neighbours, starting with the pensioner:

the pensioner next door is as fit as a flea
he burps like a pig, scares my dog and me
my dog drags his old woman off her bike
she lands in the greenhouse takes the plants for a hike[6]

His voice rasped frighteningly at the start of each verse, as if the song was an exercise in expectoration. It was surprising then that the next song was so soft, Flying Fish, written for his alter ego Tamara Danz, who had died two years earlier.

the water's like a looking glasss to you
you stare down into it and can't see me

i'll leap up for a moment into view
but any longer with you i can't be[7]

He repeated the last phrase several times, and that was the end of the concert. Gundi was exhausted but pleased with the result. He had been able to sing some of his favourite songs and intersperse them with the ideas racing through his head. They had been a captive audience.

He drove back home in the lingering daylight of the long summer evening. His diary was reasonably empty; he could relax and maybe write down some of his latest crazy ideas. It was midsummer. He could play in the garden with Linda.

Three days later Gundi drove to nearby Senftenberg, where a friend of his, a female singer, was giving a concert. She sang some of Gundi's songs. He drove home to bed. Sometime during the night he suffered a violent brain haemorrhage. Conny called the emergency services and an ambulance came. But all attempts at resuscitation failed. Gundi was dead. The doctor who examined him guessed he must have felt enormous pain, but for a mercifully short time.

twelve

. . .

Aftershock

IT WAS hard to believe that Gundi was dead at the age of forty-three. He was a singer at the height of his powers. For many east Germans he had become a people's poet. He had shaken off the shame of his Stasi past. He and his band Die Seilschaft were working well together and seemed destined for a long spell at the top.

Suddenly the earth came up to hit them. Conny was stranded in Spreetal with a six-year-old child and no clear way forward. For Die Seilschaft, as well as losing a friend they had lost their front man and songwriter—more-or-less their raison d'être. They could hardly continue to perform.

Seven days later Gundi was buried at the Forest Cemetery outside Hoyerswerda. Scores of cars choked the approach roads. Among the mourners were not only music fans, and school friends, but also dozens of Kumpels, the miners who had come to see him as their talisman, their spokesman, and even their guardian angel:

there flies an angel above the mine
  through the smoky sky

for nearly half a lifetime he's looked after me
now he's saying goodbye[1]

In September, there was a big farewell concert for Gundi at the open-air stage at Berlin-Weissensee. All his fellow musicians were there. It was a fitting send-off.

The following year BuschFunk finally released *Unplugged,* a double album of the concert that Gundermann & Seilschaft had given in 1994 with Tamara Danz and her band Silly. Both lead singers were dead, but it was a record of the finest performance the two bands had ever given together.

Through death, Gundi had grown in stature—no longer the clumsy clown, but a folk hero who had often seemed to anticipate his own early demise. Not that early, however. His own curriculum vitae, which he wrote in February 1996, predicted that he would die in 2003. At around the same time he commented in a newspaper interview:

"I've seen everything and had everything. I could go now, provided my wife Conny came with me. But that's just one side of it—having had enough. The other side is whether you're through with giving. And that's why I want to stay a little longer, at least until the children can get along without us. It's not my turn yet. If it were, I'd know it, I'd feel it. Certainly."

His song, The Future, may be closest to what he felt about his own death:

the future is just like a flying bullet
which bears my name
and which will never miss
and my thing is where's it going to land
in the head in the arse on the cheek
or in my hand
will it hit like a torpedo
or will it hit me like a kiss[2]

Midsummer's Day 2008

It was ten years since Gundi had died. Several thousand fans converged on Tempelhof a former airfield in the centre of Berlin. Near the vast terminal building—which was a relic of the Third Reich—stood a former gymnasium for US troops, the Columbiahalle. Fans crowded into the cavernous hall on a day that threatened rain. Gundermann's former band, Die Seilschaft, had come together after ten years of doing other things, while still mourning the death of their singer/songwriter. Only recently, Christian Haase, with a voice approximating Gundi's, had joined the band and begun to revive the spirit of those concerts of the 1990s. The songs were still sharp, the words just as haunting. The concert was entitled *Alle Oder Keiner* (*Everyone or No One*) after one of the songs in Gundermann's 1992 album *Einsame Spitze*. Die Seilschaft were not the only band who played. Other musicians inspired by Gundermann took the stage. Among them was the Randgruppencombo, a West German group led by Heiner Kondschak, a writer and actor/manager, formerly at the state theatre in Tübingen. He became obsessed with Gundermann's music soon after 1998 and launched the group at the State Theatre in Tübingen in 2000. It was the same venue where Gundermann & Seilschaft had played to a near-empty house in 1994.

The tenth anniversary was a time for nostalgia among an audience of mostly east Germans. Many of them still felt a wider 'Ostalgia' for the defunct, once all-embracing East German state. Gundermann had shown them a way out of depression, enabling them to see their origins and their former isolated culture as something that made them special. But the concert was also a sign that Gundermann's popularity had crossed the German-German border. The Columbiahalle was in old West, not East, Berlin.

It was more group therapy for musicians and audience than an evening of virtuoso music. For some songs all the bands played together. One figure united them: the absent Gundi. It was remarkable that such an unassuming man, who didn't regard music as his main profession, had achieved such status—as much after his death as before it. He wasn't an Elvis, nor a John Lennon. But he might have rivalled Bob Dylan if he had written and sung in English, not German.

On April 29th 2018 a small band of poetry and music lovers converged on a piece of pine forest near Taubendorf in Lusatia, which was threatened with destruction by mining. They had come to hear Udo Tiffert, a local poet and satirist, read some of his verses and Gregor Wieland Weitze perform some songs by Gerhard Gundermann.

Twenty years almost to the day since Gundi's untimely death, the rock poet and digger driver was still part of the Lausitz debate on coal mining.

René Schuster, long-serving spokesman for the Grüne Liga environmental group in Cottbus, introduced the open-air reading. Sunlight filtered through the tall fir trees. There was soft birdsong, but in the distance, plainly audible, was the rattle of the bucket-wheel diggers at work in the Jänschwalde mine.

Udo read short pieces of poetry and prose. Gregor strummed his guitar gently and sang a couple of Gundermann songs.

The little gathering showed the locals' determination to save this strip of woodland, ugly pine monoculture though it might be, as a vital barrier between the village of Taubendorf and the Jänschwalde mine.

The strains of a Gundermann song, Ought To Be, echoed through the forest, as if he were there in spirit:

the trees shall be my brothers again
we'll let our wounds repair
in the branches the birds should sing again
and with me the cherries share[3]

That summer Gundi fans in Lusatia—in fact all over east Germany—were celebrating the twentieth anniversary of the rock poet's death.

There was a six-day symposium in Hoyerswerda and nearby Grossräschen on the subject of *Gundermanns Lieder in Europa* (Gundermann's Songs in Europe). Musicians from more than ten countries presented translated versions of Gundi's songs, notably Johan Meijer a Dutchman living in Germany, and Dave Robb, a Scotsman living in Belfast. The translations spanned twelve different languages including two minority dialects: Lower Sorbian and Low German. The symposium was convened by Gundermann's fan club Gundermanns Seilschaft e.V. West German songmaker Manfred Maurenbrecher, who had briefly toured with Gundi, made a speech remembering how internationally-minded he was. He recalled a visit with him in 1992 to a favourite canal-side café in Kreuzberg, Berlin, which had a Japanese waiter and a Kurdish chef, while Russian musicians busked in the street and a couple of Italian girls flirted with their young men. Gundi loved the cultural mix which hadn't been there in former East Germany. "It fair makes your heart run over," he said.

The twentieth anniversary celebrations were followed at the end of August by the launch of a feature film called simply

Gundermann. Director Andreas Dresen had spent ten years putting together a dramatised account of Gundi's life—a controversial subject because of Gundi's short career as a Stasi collaborator. It was not clear whether Gundermann would come across as a hero or a villain.

Dresen cast Alexander Scheer as Gundi. Scheer had already made his mark as a star in *Sonnenallee*, a film about a lad coming of age in East Berlin in the 1980s. When the actor was clad in loose-fitting jeans and collarless shirt, given a pony-tail and sticky-out teeth he was almost indistinguishable from earlier footage of Gundermann as digger driver and rock singer. The film was hailed in Germany as a resounding success. Not only did it introduce Gundi's music and lyrics to new fans across the country —it broke new ground in endeavours by film-makers to portray life in eastern Germany before, during and after the fall of the Wall. Films such as *Sonnenallee*, *Goodbye Lenin* and *The Lives of Others* had each been praised in their time for getting ever closer to that perceived truth. For many in the audience the *Gundermann* film went a step further.

Soon it headed the country's DVD best-seller list. Alexander Scheer found he had a new career playing Gundermann songs, rivalling two other singers who were already established in that field: Christian Haase, with Gundermann's former band Die Seilschaft, and Heiner Kondschak with the Randgruppenkombo in Tübingen.

At the Deutscher Filmpreis in May 2019 the film swept the board with six awards including those for best feature film, best director (Andreas Dresen); best leading actor (Alexander Scheer) and best screenplay (Laila Stieler). The film reinforced Gundi's reputation as one of the most original songwriters of the twentieth century.

songs quoted in the text

chapter 1

1. ilja muromez
2. colt 08
3. fliegender fisch—flying fish

chapter 2

1. hoywoy

chapter 3

1. blau und blau — blue and blue
2. s.o.s.
3. *Egon Krenz* — (by Wenzel & Mensching)
4. brigitta

chapter 4

1. steinland—stoneland
2. dem deutschen volke —to the german people
3. die grüne armee — the green army
4. soll sein — ought to be
5. halte durch — keep going

chapter 5

1. ossi reservation—
2. ich kann mich nicht erinnern — i can't remember
3. linda
4. frühstück für immer — breakfast forever
5. sehnsucht nach dem rattenfänger — longing for the rat-catcher

chapter 6

1. der 7te samurai — the 7th samurai

chapter 7

1. vater—father

chapter 8

1. *Vergiss Nicht, Vater* — Remember, Father (by Werner Karma)
2. fliegender fisch — flying fish
3. einmal — one day
4. leine los — off the leash
5. sieglinde

chapter 9

1. krieg—war
2. hier bin ich geboren — here's where i was born
3. kommen und gehen—coming and going

chapter 10

1. engel über dem revier—angel over the mine
2. Wer hat ein helles Licht bei der Nacht — Who Holds A Bright Light In The Night

chapter 11

1. Der Narr — The Fool
2. Strasse nach Norden — The Road to the North
3. lancelots zwischenbilanz — lancelot's interim report
4. gras—grass
5. einmal — one day
6. in der nachbarschaft — in the neighbourhood
7. fliegender fisch — flying fish

chapter 12

1. engel über dem Revier — angel above the mine
2. die zukunft — the future
3. soll sein—ought to be

sources and references

Die Schmerzen der Lausitz — Documentary Film by Peter Rocha, DEFA-Studio für Trickfilme, 1989-90

Ende der Eisenzeit — Documentary Film by Richard Engel (1999)

Ernst Busch, Rio Reiser, and Gerhard Gundermann: Examples of Proletarian Narrative Role-Play in German Political Song. David Robb, Queen's University Belfast, Lied und populäre Kultur, 60/61, 227-246, 2016

Gundermann — Feature Film by Andreas Dresen, 2018

Gundermann, das Liederbuch 1 & 2 — BuschFunk Liederverlag (1996 and 1999)

Gundermanns Lieder in Europa—Symposium, Workshop & Audio CD, BuschFunk Verlag 2019

Gundermann Revier — Documentary Film by Grit Lemke, 2020

Gundermann: Von jedem Tag will ich was haben, was ich nicht vergesse, (Briefe, Dokumente, Interviews, Erinnerungen), Andreas Leusink (Herausgeber), Links Verlag, 2018

Gundi Gundermann — Documentary Film by Richard Engel (1982)

Kinder von Hoy, Grit Lemke, Suhrkamp, 2021

Tankstelle für Verlierer — Gespräche mit Gerhard Gundermann, eine Erinnerung — Hans-Dieter Schütt, Dietz, Berlin 2018

Utopia and Disillusion in the Songs of Gundermann
From the Brigade Feuerstein Productions in the GDR
to his Solo Albums (1990s), David Robb, Queen's University Belfast, 2020

about the author

David Shirreff is a writer of plays, musicals, fiction and non-fiction. He has travelled widely as a journalist for various publications including ***Euromoney***, *The Economist* and *The Wall Street Journal*.

He regards Germany as his second home, having been born there, of British parents, and having studied and worked there for many years.

After the fall of the Berlin Wall in 1989 he reported regularly from former Eastern bloc countries, including eastern Germany.

Other books by David Shirreff:

Dealing with Financial Risk, Profile Books, 2004

Don't Start From Here: We Need a Banking Revolution, Crunch Books, 2014

Vulkan — the evil empire's last gamble, a cold-war thriller, Crunch Books, 2015

Overland 1970, Crunch Books, 2022

More information at www.crunchbooks.com